CORNERSTONES OF FREEDOM™

THE SURRENDER AT APPOMATTOX

BY PETER BENOIT

CHILDREN'S PRESS®
An Imprint of Scholastic Inc.
New York Toronto London Auckland Sydney
Mexico City New Delhi Hong Kong
Danbury, Connecticut

BRINGING HISTORY to LIFE

Content Consultant
James Marten, PhD
Professor and Chair,
History Department
Marquette University
Milwaukee, Wisconsin

Library of Congress Cataloging-in-Publication Data

Benoit, Peter, 1955–
  The surrender at Appomattox/by Peter Benoit.
      p. cm.—(Cornerstones of freedom)
  Includes bibliographical references and index.
  ISBN-13: 978-0-531-25041-9 (lib. bdg.)   ISBN-10: 0-531-25041-5 (lib. bdg.)
  ISBN-13: 978-0-531-26566-6 (pbk.)   ISBN-10: 0-531-26566-8 (pbk.)
  1. Appomattox Campaign, 1865—Juvenile literature. 2. Lee, Robert E.
(Robert Edward), 1807–1870—Juvenile literature. 3. Grant, Ulysses S.
(Ulysses Simpson), 1822–1885—Juvenile literature. 4. United
States—History—Civil War, 1861-1865—Peace—Juvenile literature.
I. Title.
  E477.67.B46 2012
  973.7'38—dc22   2011011967

1 2 3 4 5 6 7 8 9 10 R 21 20 19 18 17 16 15 14 13 12

Photographs © 2012: Alamy Images/Maurice Savage: 13; AP Images/
North Wind Picture Archives: 5 top, 46, 49, 59; Art Resource, NY/Snark: 48;
Bridgeman Art Library International Ltd., London/New York: 21 (© Chicago
History Museum), 7, 47 (© Look and Learn), 12 (Alonzo Chappel/© Chicago
History Museum), 11 (Kurz & Allison/Private Collection/Peter Newark
Military Pictures), 10 (H. Charles McBarron/Private Collection/Peter Newark
Military Pictures), 8 (Henry Alexander Ogden/Private Collection/Peter
Newark American Pictures), 26, 57 bottom (Henry Alexander Ogden/Private
Collection/The Stapleton Collection); Clifford Oliver Photography/www.clif-
fordoliverphotography.com: 64; Getty Images: 24 (Buyenlarge), 55 (Hulton
Archive), 4 bottom, 42 (Stock Montage); Library of Congress: 20 (Bain
News Service), 38 (Brady National Photographic Art Gallery), 27 (Currier
& Ives), 25 (Kurz & Allison), 35 (Henry Alexander Ogden/Jones Brothers
Publishing Co.), 18 (Timothy H. O'Sullivan), 16, 40 (Thomas C. Roche), 41, 56
(Julian Vannerson), back cover, 5 bottom, 22, 29, 30, 44, 50, 57 top; National
Geographic Stock/Tom Lovell: cover; Superstock, Inc.: 32 (Dennis Malone
Carter), 17 (Everett Collection), 33 (Visions of America); The Granger
Collection, New York: 15, 58 (Matthew Brady), 2, 3, 45 (Thomas Nast), 36
(Augustus Tholey), 28, 34, 39, 51; The Image Works/Topham: 4 top, 37.

Did you know that studying history can be fun?

BRING HISTORY TO LIFE by becoming a history investigator. Examine the evidence (primary and secondary source materials); cross-examine the people and witnesses. Take a look at what was happening at the time—but be careful! What happened years ago might suddenly become incredibly interesting and change the way you think!

Contents

4

A Defining Moment in American History

Confederate general Robert E. Lee surrendered to **Union** general Ulysses S. Grant near Appomattox Court House in Virginia on April 9, 1865. The surrender effectively ended the American Civil War. Lee's decision to surrender was in doubt to the very end. The terms offered by Grant were unusual. They were meant to meet Union president Abraham Lincoln's goal. Lincoln had wanted in the closing weeks of the war to win quickly and decisively. But he especially wanted to promote a peaceful **reconciliation** between the Union and the Confederacy.

The events of that day had begun to take shape almost a year before in the bloody fighting of the Wilderness Campaign. But it was the later **siege** of Petersburg, Virginia, that laid the groundwork for Lee's surrender. The meeting of the generals on April 9 was conducted with mutual respect in the manner stated in President Lincoln's second inaugural address: "with malice toward none, with charity for all."

The Confederate capital at Richmond, Virginia, had been **evacuated** and set ablaze one week earlier. Confederate supporter John Wilkes Booth assassinated Lincoln less than a week later, on April 14. Some people feared that the conflict would be renewed. Instead, the Union was preserved. The historic meeting of Lee and Grant at Appomattox was at the center of that outcome.

Confederate general Robert E. Lee (right) surrendered to Union general Ulysses S. Grant at Appomattox Court House, Virginia.

OF A MAN NAMED WILMER MCLEAN.

CHAPTER 1

THE HORRORS OF WAR

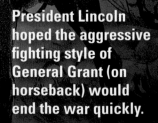

President Lincoln hoped the aggressive fighting style of General Grant (on horseback) would end the war quickly.

THE WILDERNESS CAMPAIGN

was a series of battles fought in Virginia's scrub oak and pine forest in May and June 1864. It marked the beginning of an important strategic shift in the Union army's war plans. President Lincoln had been impressed by General Ulysses S. Grant's success in the siege of Vicksburg, Mississippi, the previous summer. Lincoln put Grant in overall command of the Union army in March 1864.

Grant quickly established a broad war plan that would strike at several key strategic points. General George G. Meade would lead the Army of the Potomac in Virginia. Meade and his men would work to defeat Robert E. Lee's Army of Northern Virginia and capture the Confederate capital at Richmond.

SPOTLIGHT ON

The Siege of Vicksburg

Control of the Mississippi River was an important objective for the Union army. Vicksburg, Mississippi, was a critical location along the river. It also sat directly in the middle of the Confederacy. By taking Vicksburg, the Union would gain control of the river and split the Confederacy in half. Grant attempted to take the city on May 19 and May 22, 1863. But Confederate forces turned him back. The Union had heavy **casualties**. Grant's army then surrounded the city. They blocked supplies from coming in. Vicksburg surrendered on July 4. The victory gave the Union the upper hand in the rest of the war.

The Wilderness Campaign resulted in heavy losses to both armies. But Grant had twice as many troops. He stood to win if he could force Lee into a showdown. But Union success was not guaranteed. Lee had won a stunning victory in the area the previous year at Chancellorsville. Reminders of that battle were apparent when the Battle of the Wilderness began on May 5. There were skulls on the forest floor. Decayed limbs wrapped in blue and gray uniforms poked up out of shallow graves.

During the Battle of the Wilderness, thick clouds of gun smoke and **artillery** fire made it impossible for soldiers to communicate. Any organized battle plan was quickly forgotten. Artillery shells set the underbrush on fire. This engulfed the soldiers in a sea of flames. Both sides had heavy losses. Grant lost about 17,500 men in the two days of fighting.

The Battle of the Wilderness was one of the most gruesome battles of the Civil War.

Lee lost about 11,000. But Grant stayed on the offensive. He pursued his enemy in battle after battle as he had promised President Lincoln he would.

The next battle of the campaign was at Spotsylvania. It began on May 8. The men fought hand to hand for an entire day. Attacks and counterattacks continued for several days. Casualties mounted on both sides. Grant's decision to attack strong Confederate defensive positions caused a horrific loss of life. His critics labeled him a "butcher."

The two armies now raced to Cold Harbor. Cold Harbor was less than 10 miles (16 kilometers) from

The Battle of Spotsylvania in Virginia was fought between May 8 and May 21, 1864.

Richmond. Grant ordered another attack. More brutal combat followed. Seven thousand more Union soldiers lay dead at the end of the day.

Grant had suffered the loss of more than 50,000 troops during the first month of the Wilderness Campaign. But there was no rest for the Army of the Potomac. Grant marched them south to the banks of the James River. He hoped to cross the river and seize the railroad junction at Petersburg. Lee's worst nightmare was about to begin.

Petersburg was only about 20 miles (32 km) from Richmond. Lee mistakenly believed that the capital was Grant's next

TODAY'S PERSPECTIVE

Modern military historians understand that the siege of Petersburg was a thoughtfully designed campaign. The siege did not involve Grant's forces completely surrounding Petersburg. They instead combined **trench warfare** with strategies designed to stretch and thin Confederate lines until defense was impossible. Soldiers fought from long, narrow ditches. These ditches offered them protection during the fighting. The siege lasted from June 1864 to March 1865. Lee's army was not destroyed and Richmond was not captured. But the siege ultimately led to Lee's retreat and a series of battles called the Appomattox Campaign that ended the Civil War.

objective. As a result, he sent only a few troops to defend Petersburg. They were led by General Pierre Beauregard. Grant knew that control of Petersburg threatened the Confederate capital because railroad supply lines through Petersburg led directly to Richmond. Grant did not attempt to completely surround Petersburg. He instead controlled rail lines to limit the flow of supplies to Lee's army.

Lee's army lived in 37 miles (60 km) of trenches stretching from southwest of Petersburg to east of Richmond. Grant's Army of the Potomac was larger and better supplied than Lee's forces. They launched several attacks against Lee's army between July and October 1864. Grant's forces almost always suffered heavier losses. But the Union army was able to survive the losses because they were better equipped and more numerous.

Union troops huddle together in a trench at Petersburg, Virginia, in December 1864.

Misery

Lincoln had imposed a naval **blockade** on Confederate ports at the beginning of the war. The blockade had taken a heavy toll on the South. Southern states could no longer sell and ship goods such as cotton and tobacco to Great Britain. The Confederacy was unable to keep up with the costs of fighting the war because of this. The Confederacy printed more money. But the money's value had decreased, making ordinary goods

Many soldiers were killed in the deep trenches they had dug for protection at Petersburg.

unaffordable. Food shortages were common. Grant's army did not always threaten the railways. But supplies to the Confederates in Petersburg failed to arrive anyway. Many soldiers lacked overcoats, blankets, and food.

Disease was common at Petersburg. The men suffered from lice. Rats ran everywhere. They scurried over the bodies of soldiers who had died from disease. Wounds became infected. Limbs often had to be **amputated** to prevent people from dying. The Confederates' misery was made worse by the constant explosion of Union artillery shells. There seemed to be no end in sight to the soldiers' suffering.

Frustration in the South mounted. People debated freeing slaves and allowing them to join the Confederate army. Lee himself grew increasingly frustrated with the Confederate Congress. He felt they were not responding to the crisis in the trenches. Lee's soldiers began to leave their posts in large numbers by February 1865.

Only 35,000 soldiers remained in the Army of Northern Virginia by March. Meanwhile, Grant had almost 150,000 men. Lee knew Grant could eventually be reinforced with more Union troops. He was faced with surrender or defeat. Lee knew that his army could no longer defend the Confederate capital. Another strategy would be necessary. Confederate major general John Gordon had a plan.

Confederate soldiers were generally less well equipped than Union soldiers.

CHAPTER 2

THE RISE AND FALL OF FORTUNE

STEDMAN.

The Confederate attack on Fort Stedman was a final attempt to break the Union siege at Petersburg.

THREE GROUPS OF 100

Confederate soldiers each went out into the darkness to **probe** Grant's line at 4:15 a.m. on March 25. More than 12,000 troops in the Confederate **infantry** soon sprang into action and confronted the startled Union troops in hand-to-hand combat. Lee's infantry shortly took control of Fort Stedman and nearly 1 mile (1.6 km) of Union trenches. Then the Union counterattack began.

YESTERDAY'S HEADLINES

George F. Williams was a *New York Times* war correspondent reporting from the Battle of Fort Stedman. He wrote, "There is no use speculating [wondering] in regard to any ultimate result arising out of this aggressive movement on the part of Gen. Lee, for no one can tell what may come of it." In 1884, Williams wrote a book entitled *Bullet and Shell: The Civil War as the Soldier Saw It.* It was based on his experiences as a war correspondent and soldier in the New York Volunteers unit during the Civil War.

Lee's infantry was driven back almost immediately by an astonishing show of firepower. Lee's army had been reduced by almost 5,000 troops within hours. The fort was regained by the Union. Lee's hopes for defending Richmond had vanished.

He reported to Confederate president Jefferson Davis that Richmond would soon fall to the Union. Lee knew his only hope was in marching south and joining forces with General Joseph Johnston in North Carolina. The siege of Petersburg was over.

Lincoln Meets with His Generals

Lincoln was encouraged by Grant's defense of Fort Stedman. He quickly arranged a visit to the battlefield the same day. The trip would provide Lincoln an

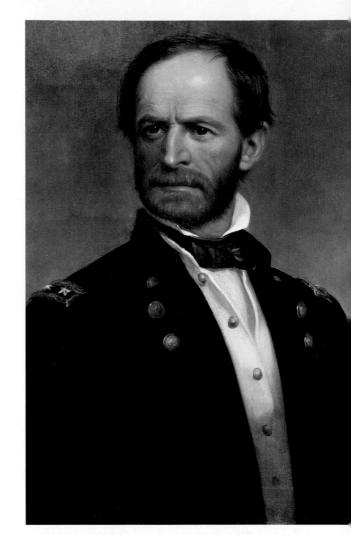

General William Tecumseh Sherman was one of President Lincoln's most trusted military leaders.

opportunity to discuss a new assault on Petersburg with his top military leaders. Grant, General William Tecumseh Sherman, and Rear Admiral David Dixon Porter met with Lincoln aboard Grant's steamship, the *River Queen*. It was afloat in the Potomac.

Lincoln and Secretary of State

A FIRSTHAND LOOK AT
FORT STEDMAN

Harper's Weekly of April 15, 1865, provided battlefield sketches of the crucial Battle of Fort Stedman. *Harper's* was a steady source of reporting and sketches for a public that wanted to better understand the conflict. The surrender at Appomattox was almost a week old by the time the sketches were published. See page 60 for a link to view the sketches.

Rear Admiral David Dixon Porter fought in several major sea battles during the war and helped improve the U.S. Navy's fighting ability.

William Seward had met with three representatives of the Confederacy in February to negotiate an end to the war. The four-hour meeting had also been held on the *River Queen*. It had ended with no progress being made. Lincoln now listened as his generals expressed their fears that Lee would slip away and join up with Johnston.

Lincoln wondered how to justify continuing this brutal conflict without harming his larger goal of healing

the nation's divisions and saving the Union. He proposed that generous terms of surrender be arranged when the war ended. Lincoln told his officers, "Let them all go, officers and all, I want submission, and no more bloodshed . . . I want no one punished; treat them liberally all around. We want those people to return to their allegiance to the Union and submit to the laws."

Lincoln had arrived for the conference with his generals by train. He had seen Confederate prisoners bloodied and

A VIEW FROM ABROAD

Abraham Lincoln wrestled with the problem of ending the war decisively and then joining North and South together in harmony. Lincoln announced the Emancipation Proclamation at the beginning of 1863. It freed most of the slaves in the country. Lincoln issued it partly to shift the balance of war in the Union's favor. Freed slaves could be trained to fight for the Union. Some observers in Great Britain claimed that Lincoln's true motive for the proclamation was to destroy the Confederacy from within by encouraging slave riots. But none of Lincoln's speeches, correspondences, or official actions ever expressed such an aim.

exhausted as he passed the battlefield. Now he heard the steady boom of artillery and saw the lightning flashes of war from the deck of the *River Queen*. The final assault on Petersburg had begun.

An original map of the Battle of Five Forks shows the positions of Union and Confederate forces.

The Chase

The Battle of Five Forks was fought southwest of Petersburg on April 1. It was the beginning of the end for Lee's army and the Confederacy. The Confederate **cavalry** and Confederate general George Pickett's infantry had fought against Union general Philip Sheridan's troops the previous day at Dinwiddie Court House. The Confederates had successfully slowed Sheridan's advance. Lee now commanded them to hold the crossroads at Five Forks.

Opportunities for Lee's army to retreat were disappearing. The evacuation of Richmond was a certainty. It was only hours away. The Fifth Corps of the Union army would soon reinforce Sheridan's troops. Pickett's defense was crushed by the Union forces.

Lee telegraphed General James Longstreet to come at once. But Longstreet was more than half a day away. He would not arrive in time. Grant was aware of Lee's situation. He launched a full-scale artillery attack on Lee's lines south of the Appomattox River in the early morning hours of April 2. The Union infantry quickly poured into the holes created in Lee's lines. Lee had been meeting with General A. P. Hill and heard the roar of battle coming near. He walked out into the darkness and saw wagons approaching. They were barely half a

The fighting at the Battle of Five Forks forced General Lee to give up his positions at Petersburg and move toward Appomattox.

General Philip H. Sheridan commanded the Union forces at Five Forks.

mile (1 km) away. It was Sheridan's army. Thousands of men were charging up the hill.

Cannons were rolled into position and began firing at the advancing Union forces. Lee telegraphed his generals and told them to hold Petersburg until he could evacuate. He sent an emergency message to Jefferson Davis warning him to clear out of Richmond that night. Lee's headquarters was struck by a shell moments later. It ignited a fire. Lee mounted his gray horse, Traveller, and sped out at top speed. His headquarters burned to the ground. The chase had begun.

Richmond Is Burning

Jefferson Davis sat quietly in St. Paul's Episcopal Church on April 2. The only sounds disturbing the peaceful morning were those of distant artillery explosions and the tolling of church bells. A messenger slipped in and waited for the proper moment to deliver Lee's telegram. Davis's face went white as he read it slowly. He got up and rushed from the church.

Richmond quickly responded to the news. People prepared to evacuate the city before nightfall. Important government documents were loaded on a train heading to Danville, Virginia. There, the Confederacy would establish

Fires were started in Richmond, both by looters and by city officials burning government documents.

Fire destroyed huge sections of Richmond as winds spread the flames from building to building.

its capital for the remainder of the war. Other documents were piled on the sidewalks and burned. Citizens were filled with fear. They wondered if they would be hanged for **treason** if captured. Many packed up what they could carry and left. Others held on to the city they loved. They closed their shutters as night fell.

The **militia** destroyed weapons so they wouldn't fall into the hands of Union troops. They also set tobacco warehouses on fire and sank abandoned naval vessels. But winds spread the fire later in the evening. It burned out of control and set homes, churches, and factories ablaze. Buildings collapsed. Mobs of convicts roamed the streets.

More than 100,000 artillery shells that had been stored at the National **Arsenal** blew up when the fire reached them. The streets were as bright as day in the middle of the night. The city was mostly rubble by the morning. Lee and his starving Confederate soldiers had already begun their desperate 40-mile (64 km) march westward to Amelia Court House. A railroad car full of supplies was to be waiting for them. They had almost a full day's lead on Grant's army. But another surprise was waiting for Lee as he moved farther from Richmond.

As the Confederate capital lay in ruins, General Lee marched away to distance his forces from the Union army.

CHAPTER 3

THE HEAVENS TURNED UPSIDE DOWN

Union soldiers came upon a scene of near-total destruction when they entered Richmond on April 3.

UNION TROOPS SWEPT
toward the abandoned Confederate capital on the
morning of April 3. A scene of utter devastation
awaited them. A Union corps made up entirely of
African Americans was the first to enter the city.
They were immediately asked to restore order
and help put out the fires that still burned. More
Union regiments poured into Richmond. Their
bands played "The Star Spangled Banner." The
U.S. flag was put on flagpoles. Families huddled
in smoke-filled streets as their homes burned. The
conquering Union army turned Jefferson Davis's
mansion into a military headquarters.

Large crowds happily greeted President Lincoln as he walked through the burned-out streets of Richmond.

"Father Abraham"

President Lincoln was nearby at City Point with his son Tad when he heard the news of Richmond's capture. The two boarded the *Malvern* and steamed to Richmond. Lincoln strolled through the city toward Jefferson Davis's home on April 4. He was dressed in a long black coat and high silk hat. Slaves and freedmen looked on from broken-down shacks. A few came into the street, then thousands more. Tears streamed down their faces. They cried, "Glory hallelujah!" They approached the president and strained to touch his clothing and his hands. An elderly woman shouted, "I know I am free, for I have seen Father Abraham and felt him."

Lincoln finally arrived at Davis's mansion. He wasted no time sitting in Davis's chair. He seemed strangely at peace. Lincoln met with Union general Godfrey Weitzel, Confederate general Richard Heron Anderson, and others. Lincoln instructed Weitzel how the Union army was to behave. He also offered assurances of peaceful reconciliation to Anderson.

YESTERDAY'S HEADLINES

On April 4, the *New York Times* ran a commentary on "The President's Visit to Richmond." Its tone sternly questioned why Lincoln would risk his personal safety by walking so casually through the streets of Richmond. A guard of 10 sailors accompanied him. But the *Times* believed Lincoln was selfishly satisfying his own curiosity by walking among the slaves and freedmen. Of course, his visit had a very deep and profound meaning to the freed slaves.

Confederate president Jefferson Davis fled Richmond on April 2, only one day before Union troops entered the city.

A Human Story

Lee's troops streamed from the trenches of Petersburg in darkness. They pressed forward to Amelia Court House in four large groups. One group was already south of the Appomattox River. It only needed to continue westward to the rail yards of Amelia Court House and its promised boxcars of supplies. The other three would have to cross the river on one of three bridges.

But Bevils Bridge had been washed out by recent heavy rains. Genito Bridge would be unable to support the weight of thousands of marching troops, horses, and loaded wagons. Some of Lee's army began to push over the one remaining bridge. Others looked for ways to get across on railroads downstream. This took valuable time away from the fleeing Confederates. It gave the Union forces time to close the distance between the two armies.

The Union cavalry attacked Confederate infantrymen at the rear. They engaged in brief fights almost constantly at Sutherland Station on the first day of the escape. The fighting grew more intense on the second day. The Confederates used farmhouses as hospitals. They treated their wounded as the Army of Northern

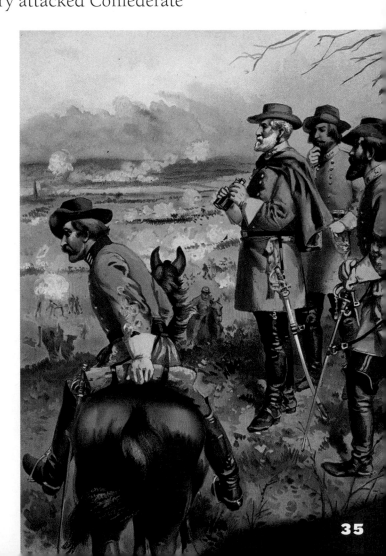

Lee (center, standing) was on the run in April 1865.

Virginia pressed on to Amelia Court House and the promise of supplies. The Confederates had only brought enough food for one day. But they were now heading into the third day of their journey.

The boxcars came into view on April 5. Lee and his faithful troops looked on as they were opened. There was ammunition and artillery but no food. Lee sent men and wagons out to nearby farms to beg for food. But

The leaders of the Confederate army were well-trained, experienced soldiers, but they ran out of food.

General Grant (center, in brimmed hat) and his men pursued the retreating Confederate forces for two weeks.

the men returned empty-handed. The food shortages of recent months had left nothing. Lee's troops had lost valuable time. Their carefully crafted plan had unraveled.

A FIRSTHAND LOOK AT
GENERAL GRANT'S PURSUIT OF GENERAL LEE

A message from General Grant was forwarded to the *New York Times*. It appeared in the April 5, 1865, paper. The message describes the heavy losses taken by Lee's retreating army: "Houses through the country are nearly all used as hospitals for wounded men." Describing his own cavalry, Grant continues, "The cavalry have pursued so closely that the enemy have been forced to destroy . . . transportation, caissons [wheeled vehicles that hold ammunition], and munitions of war. . . . I shall continue the pursuit as long as there appears to be any use in it." See page 60 for a link to review Grant's words reprinted in *Harper's Weekly* on April 15, 1865.

Lee hoped to join forces with General Joseph Johnston (pictured) in North Carolina.

The Union cavalry learned that Lee had requested supply wagons to arrive 7 miles (11 km) northwest of Amelia Court House. They burned the wagons. The two armies then battled once more. This further drained the Confederates. Lee turned his army toward Burkeville. But the Union cavalry was backed by the infantry. They had established a blockade near Jetersville. They now controlled the road. Lee's hopes for escape were falling apart.

The average Confederate soldier was between 21 and 23 years old.

Hard Choices

Lee turned west toward Lynchburg as a downpour of rain turned dirt roads to soft muck. His men were exhausted and hungry. They grew confused. Mules could not pull their loads through the mud. Men drank from puddles and tore the bark from trees to eat. They pushed on to Farmville and a promise of small amounts of food. Fighting broke out near Sayler's Creek on April 6. Some Confederates were out of ammunition. They ran into the

The four terrible years of the Civil War caused more than 600,000 deaths and massive destruction.

spray of gunfire with only knives and empty guns. The fighting continued for hours. Thousands of soldiers were killed, captured, or wounded.

The Confederates reached Farmville on the morning of April 7. They rested there and ate what little food a supply train was able to deliver. The Union cavalry and infantry arrived as they paused to eat. Furious fighting broke out in the streets of Farmville. The supply train was ruined. Thousands of men had not yet received their food. Those strong enough to flee ran across burning bridges as Union soldiers pursued them.

Grant wrote a letter to Lee. He had it delivered to Lee's camp that night by a special task force. Some of the task force were pinned down by heavy gunfire and killed. But Lee received Grant's letter. It raised the issue of a Confederate surrender. Lee knew surrender was not acceptable to his generals. He asked Grant for the terms of the proposed surrender. Robert E. Lee was about to make one of the most important decisions in the history of the United States.

Robert E. Lee

Two of Robert E. Lee's ancestors, Richard Henry and Francis Lightfoot Lee, signed the Declaration of Independence. His father, Henry "Light-Horse Harry" Lee, was a distinguished military leader and associate of George Washington. But Harry Lee fell desperately in **debt** and eventually fled to the West Indies. He left six-year-old Robert fatherless. Lee attended the West Point military academy as a young man. He graduated second in his class. At 24, he married the great-granddaughter of Martha Washington. He had restored his family's wealth by age 28.

CHAPTER 4

SURRENDER BECOMES CERTAIN

General Lee waged war against Union forces until it became obvious that a Confederate victory was impossible.

GRANT SENT ANOTHER LETTER

to Lee on April 8. It assured the Confederate leader of his desire for peace. His only demand was that members of the Army of Northern Virginia "be disqualified for taking up arms." This suggested that the Confederates would not be charged with treason against the United States.

Lee asked to meet the following morning to discuss peace. But Grant sensed that Lee still wanted to fight. He prepared for another day of combat. Grant sent a response. But it was not received before Lee's army launched an attack just outside Appomattox Court House on April 9. Lee's troops stood frozen in horror as countless Union infantrymen emerged from the woods. Lee was certain his troops would be destroyed. He at last agreed to meet with Grant.

Ulysses S. Grant

The early life of Ulysses Grant gave no indications of future abilities. He spent his days on his father's farmlands and became a talented horseman. Grant's father secured a West Point position for his son. Young Grant was 17 years old but barely 5 feet (1.5 meters) tall when he entered the military academy. He was not a great student. He graduated 21st in a class of 39 students. But he displayed a strong fighting spirit in the Mexican-American War (1846–1848). After his war service, Grant was appointed to the newly created position of general of the Army of the United States. He was elected the 18th president of the United States in 1868.

Surrender

The meeting would take place near Appomattox Court House on April 9. They met in the house owned by a man named Wilmer McLean.

Lee and his generals arrived first. Lee was well groomed and cleanly dressed in a nearly new uniform and boots. He wore a sword of exquisite craftsmanship at his side. Grant was 43 years old. He was 15 years younger than Lee. He was dressed more casually. His single-breasted suit of dark blue flannel was unbuttoned. His boots were splattered with mud.

Grant opened the conversation in a friendly tone. The Union general understood the emotional cost of the meeting for Lee. He already had great respect for the Confederate leader.

After years battling one another, Grant (left) and Lee finally met in the peaceful surroundings of Appomattox Court House.

Grant hoped to ease into their serious discussion of surrender. He began by talking about a brief meeting between the two about 20 years earlier during the Mexican-American War.

A FIRSTHAND LOOK AT
THE WAR'S END

Secretary of War Edwin M. Stanton sent out an official notice dated "April 9, 1865— 9 o'clock p.m." announcing the surrender at Appomattox. Printed in the *New York Times* the following day, the headline read, "Hang Out Your Banners: Union Victory! Peace!" At the end of his message, Stanton promised, "Details will be given as speedily as possible." See page 60 for a link to view the newspaper.

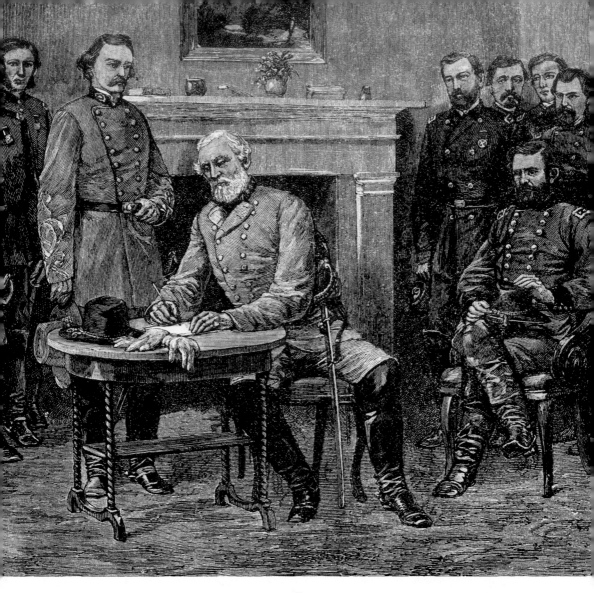

Following President Lincoln's instructions, the final terms of surrender did not harshly punish or humiliate the Confederacy.

Finally, Lee brought the discussion to the issue of surrender. Grant offered the same terms as before. Lee's men would not be jailed or tried for treason. The men must surrender their weapons and agree not to take them up against the Union again. They could take the horses they had back to their homes to help with the spring planting. Grant would also supply food for Lee's 28,000 hungry men.

A formal document detailing the agreement was drawn up in Grant's order book. Lee read it carefully. He then wrote a letter accepting the terms. Lee got up and shook Grant's hand. He then walked out the door and down the front steps of the McLean house. He paused on his way and looked sadly toward the distant valley where his army was camped. Lee delivered his final address to the Army of Northern Virginia the following day. He bid them an "affectionate farewell" and thanked them for their "duty faithfully performed."

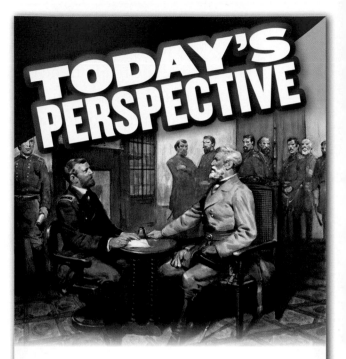

TODAY'S PERSPECTIVE

An editorial written by L. L. Crounse, appearing in the *New York Times* on April 10, 1865, expressed how unimaginable the surrender and conclusion of the war was to people of the time. His words may seem like an enormous exaggeration to us today. But they hold a basic truth that is still valid even from our 21st-century perspective. Crounse described the end of a war that tore apart the nation and took the lives of more than 620,000 soldiers. He wrote, "It is almost beyond the power of the human mind to comprehend its extent, and when you begin to descend to detail, the task is simply appalling in its magnitude."

A ceremony of formal surrender of weapons was held along the road on the edge of town on April 12. Union officer Joshua Chamberlain led the ceremony. His Confederate counterpart was Major General John Gordon. Chamberlain signaled his bugler to sound the order to carry arms. Tens of thousands of Union soldiers raised their muskets to their shoulders. General Gordon called on his men to do the same. Twenty-eight thousand Confederate soldiers surrendered guns, bayonets, and cartridges over the next seven hours. As news of Lee's surrender spread, other Confederates laid down their guns in the following weeks.

Many Confederate soldiers were sorry to hear about Lee's surrender to Grant.

Head-Quarters, *Appomattox C.H. Va.*

Apl. 9th   1865, 4.30 o'clock, *P.* M.

Hon. E. M. Stanton, Sec. of War Washington

Gen. Lee surrendered the Army of Northern Va this afternoon on terms proposed by myself. The accompanying additional correspondence will show the conditions fully.

U. S. Grant
Lt. Gen.

By Command of

General Grant sent Secretary of War Edwin Stanton this note informing him that Lee had surrendered.

Aftermath

Bells of celebration rang in small villages and great cities in many parts of the nation in the days after the surrender. All eyes turned toward Abraham Lincoln. He had been sworn in for a second term as president in early March. The weight of war was now lifted from his shoulders. Lincoln decided to attend a play called

President Lincoln and his wife, Mary, sat in these box seats above the stage when they attended the play at Ford's Theatre.

Our American Cousin at Ford's Theatre on April 14 in Washington, D.C.

Actor and Confederate supporter John Wilkes Booth snuck into Lincoln's box with a gun in his hand. He fired into the back of the president's head from close range. Lincoln died the next day. The celebrations of the previous week fell silent as the nation mourned the loss of its leader.

Booth was captured and shot trying to escape a burning barn. Another Confederate supporter sabotaged the steamboat *Sultana* on May 1. This caused a boiler explosion that killed 1,500 former Union prisoners being returned from Confederate prison camps. Though armies were returning home, bitterness still lived in many hearts. Lincoln's plan for peaceful reconciliation would take place gradually as bonds of respect for the law and for common goals were reestablished.

John Wilkes Booth fled the theater after shooting President Lincoln.

What Happened Where?

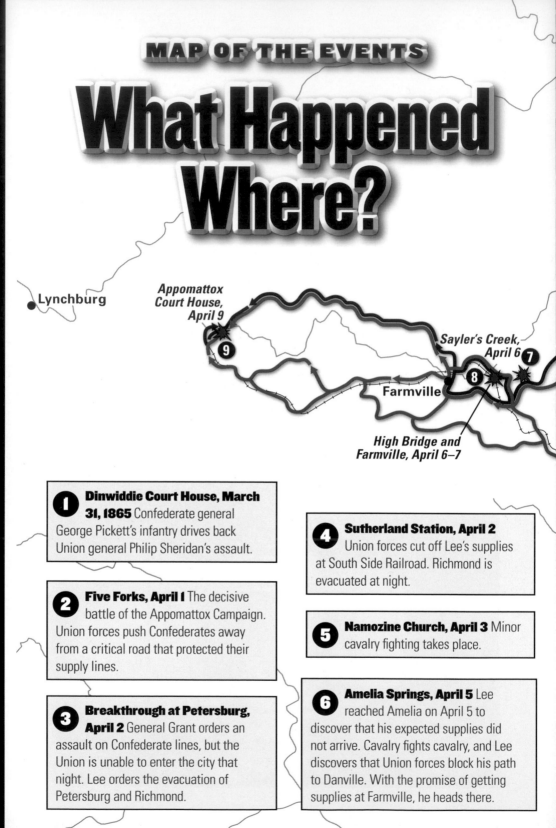

Lynchburg

Appomattox Court House, April 9

Sayler's Creek, April 6

Farmville

High Bridge and Farmville, April 6–7

1 **Dinwiddie Court House, March 31, 1865** Confederate general George Pickett's infantry drives back Union general Philip Sheridan's assault.

2 **Five Forks, April 1** The decisive battle of the Appomattox Campaign. Union forces push Confederates away from a critical road that protected their supply lines.

3 **Breakthrough at Petersburg, April 2** General Grant orders an assault on Confederate lines, but the Union is unable to enter the city that night. Lee orders the evacuation of Petersburg and Richmond.

4 **Sutherland Station, April 2** Union forces cut off Lee's supplies at South Side Railroad. Richmond is evacuated at night.

5 **Namozine Church, April 3** Minor cavalry fighting takes place.

6 **Amelia Springs, April 5** Lee reached Amelia on April 5 to discover that his expected supplies did not arrive. Cavalry fights cavalry, and Lee discovers that Union forces block his path to Danville. With the promise of getting supplies at Farmville, he heads there.

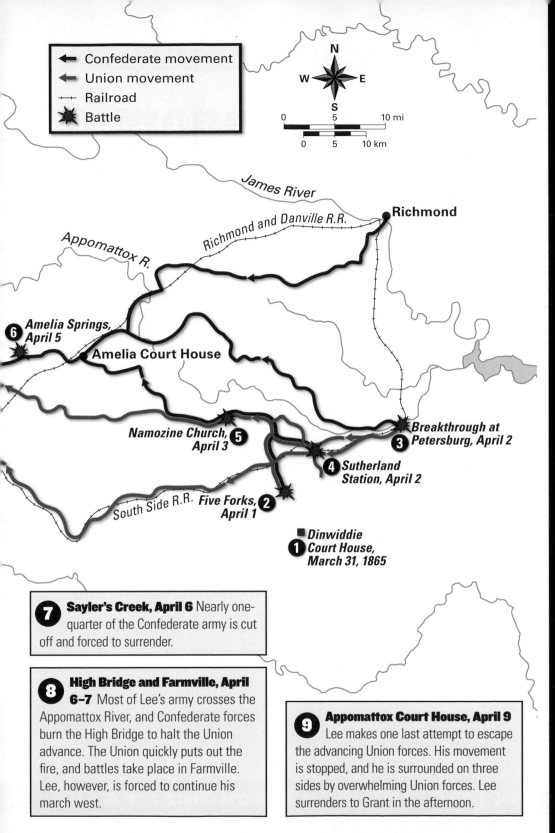

Confederate movement
Union movement
Railroad
Battle

James River

Richmond

Richmond and Danville R.R.

Appomattox R.

6 *Amelia Springs, April 5*

Amelia Court House

Namozine Church, **5** *April 3*

Breakthrough at **3** *Petersburg, April 2*

4 *Sutherland Station, April 2*

South Side R.R. *Five Forks,* **2** *April 1*

Dinwiddie **1** *Court House, March 31, 1865*

7 **Sayler's Creek, April 6** Nearly one-quarter of the Confederate army is cut off and forced to surrender.

8 **High Bridge and Farmville, April 6–7** Most of Lee's army crosses the Appomattox River, and Confederate forces burn the High Bridge to halt the Union advance. The Union quickly puts out the fire, and battles take place in Farmville. Lee, however, is forced to continue his march west.

9 **Appomattox Court House, April 9** Lee makes one last attempt to escape the advancing Union forces. His movement is stopped, and he is surrounded on three sides by overwhelming Union forces. Lee surrenders to Grant in the afternoon.

Let Freedom Ring

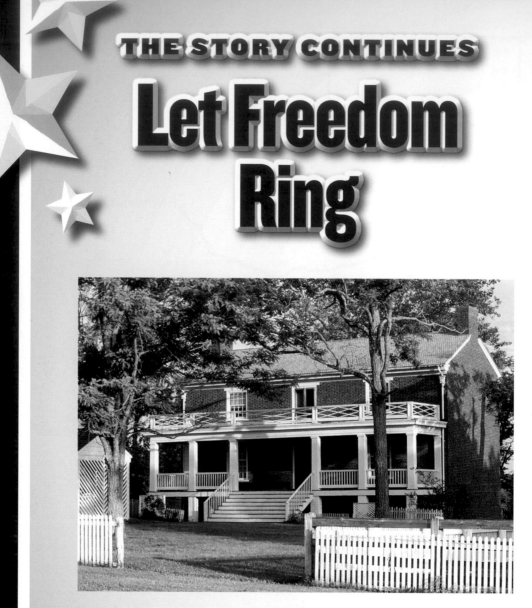

The site of the surrender still stands today and is open to visitors.

Hundreds of thousands of American lives were lost in the Civil War. Cities were turned to rubble and families were torn apart to eliminate slavery from American soil. Many questioned how a nation founded on principles

IN 1870, THE 15TH AMENDMENT GAVE

of liberty and equality could deny those ideals to four million African Americans. But with the Union victory, the Emancipation Proclamation, and the 13th Amendment to the U.S. Constitution—which officially abolished slavery—change was arriving. But it wouldn't be until the civil rights movement of the1950s and 1960s that equality for all would begin to be realized.

The gifts of liberty exist because millions of brave Americans were willing to pay for it with their lives. Much of what is often taken for granted in America today would not exist without that sacrifice 150 years ago. Generals Grant and Lee served as examples to their nation in their own time and ever since. In the handshake of Grant and Lee came a message of freedom.

Generals Lee and Grant parted ways knowing that the larger task of healing the nation's wounds lay in the years ahead.

AFRICAN AMERICAN MEN VOTING RIGHTS.

INFLUENTIAL INDIVIDUALS

Robert E. Lee

Robert E. Lee (1807–1870) was the Confederate commander of the Army of Northern Virginia. He surrendered to General Grant in 1865, ending the Civil War.

Joseph Johnston (1807–1891) was the Confederate commander of the Army of Northern Virginia before Lee. He commanded the Army of Tennessee during the Petersburg siege and the Appomattox Campaign.

Jefferson Davis (1808–1889) was president of the Confederate States of America.

Abraham Lincoln (1809–1865) was the 16th president of the United States, leading the nation through the Civil War. He was assassinated by John Wilkes Booth five days after the Confederate surrender at Appomattox.

David Dixon Porter (1813–1891) was a Union navy admiral who was important in the siege of Vicksburg, supporting Grant's successful campaign to gain control of the Mississippi River.

Wilmer McLean (1814–1882) moved from Bull Run to Appomattox Court House to escape the fury of the war. His house was the site of the signing of the surrender agreement on April 9, 1865.

William Tecumseh Sherman (1820–1891) was a Union general in the Army of Tennessee.

Ulysses S. Grant (1822–1885) was commander of the Union army from March 1864 to April 1865. A rugged and determined leader in battle, he would serve as U.S. president from 1869 to 1877.

George Pickett (1825–1875) was a Confederate general in the Army of Northern Virginia who fought at the Battle of Dinwiddie Court House and the Battle of Five Forks.

Ulysses S. Grant

Joshua Chamberlain (1828–1914) was a Union brigadier general who led the ceremony of the formal surrender of weapons at the end of the Civil War.

Philip Sheridan (1831–1888) was the U.S. Cavalry Corps commander of the Army of the Potomac. He fought in the Battle of Dinwiddie Court House and commanded the Union forces at the Battle of Five Forks.

Philip Sheridan

John Gordon (1832–1904) was important in the Confederate successes during the Wilderness Campaign and led the last Confederate charge at the Battle of Appomattox Court House.

John Wilkes Booth (1838–1865) was an actor and Confederate supporter who shot and killed President Lincoln.

TIMELINE

1864

March
Ulysses S. Grant is put in command of the Union army.

May–June
The Wilderness Campaign is waged in Virginia.

1864–1865

June 9, 1864–March 25, 1865
The nine-month siege of Petersburg is waged.

1865

March 25
The Battle of Fort Stedman is fought.

April 1
The Battle of Five Forks is fought.

April 2
Richmond is evacuated.

April 3
The Union army occupies Richmond.

April 4
President Abraham Lincoln visits Richmond.

April 5
The Battle of Amelia Springs is fought.

April 6
The Battle of Sayler's Creek is fought.

April 7
Grant offers Robert E. Lee terms of surrender.

April 9
The Battle of Appomattox Court House is fought; surrender meeting takes place at the McLean house.

April 10
Lee makes a farewell address to his troops.

April 12
The Confederate surrender of arms ceremony takes place.

April 14
Abraham Lincoln is shot at Ford's Theatre.

April 15
Lincoln dies.

LIVING HISTORY

Primary sources provide firsthand evidence about a topic. Witnesses to a historical event create primary sources. They include autobiographies, newspaper reports of the time, oral histories, photographs, and memoirs. A secondary source analyzes primary sources, and is one step or more removed from the event. Secondary sources include textbooks, encyclopedias, and commentaries.

Announcing the End of the War To see the original *New York Times* edition that featured Secretary of War Edwin M. Stanton's declaration that the war had ended, go to *www.nytimes.com/learning/general/onthisday/big/0409.html*

Fort Stedman To view sketches of battlefield action at Fort Stedman, go to *www.sonofthesouth.net/leefoundation/civil-war/1865/April/fort-steadman-battle.htm*

General Grant's Pursuit of General Lee To read General Grant's message about his pursuit of General Lee that appeared in the *New York Times* and *Harper's Weekly*, go to *www.sonofthesouth.net/leefoundation/civil-war/1865/April/general-winthrop-death.htm*

"Public Impatience About Military Movements" To view the *New York Times* editorial urging readers to be more patient regarding the Union's seemingly slow, frustrating progress in the war, see *www.nytimes.com/1864/06/22/news/public-impatience-about-military-movements.html?scp=27&sq=june+22%2C+1864&st=p*

RESOURCES

Books

Brager, Bruce. *Petersburg*. New York: Chelsea House Publications, 2002.

Houghton, Gillian. *Grant and Lee at Appomattox: A Primary Source History of the End of the Civil War*. New York: Rosen, 2004.

Kantor, MacKinlay. *Lee and Grant at Appomattox*. New York: Sterling, 2007.

Swanson, James L. *Chasing Lincoln's Killer*. New York: Scholastic Press, 2009.

Web Sites

Appomattox Court House
www.nps.gov/apco/index.htm
Visit the McLean house where Lee surrendered to Grant and view the site of the final fighting of the Civil War.

Civil War Trust
www.civilwar.org/education/students/kidswebsites.html
One of the best Civil War sources on the Web. Be sure to check out the special sections on battles, biographies, strategies, maps, photos, and primary sources.

Georgia's Blue and Gray Trail Presents America's Civil War
http://blueandgraytrail.com/event/Surrender_Letters
Georgia's Historic High Country Travel Association site provides scores of links relating to the war, including an amazing war encyclopedia and the letters of surrender exchanged by Grant and Lee at Appomattox.

GLOSSARY

amputated (AM-pyuh-tayt-ed) removed a damaged limb, finger, or toe by cutting it off

arsenal (AR-suh-nuhl) a place where weapons and ammunition are stored

artillery (ahr-TIL-ur-ee) large, powerful weapons such as cannons

blockade (blah-KAYD) a closing off of an area, such as a port, to keep supplies from going in or out

casualties (KAZH-oo-uhl-teez) people killed or wounded during warfare

cavalry (KAV-uhl-ree) soldiers mounted on horseback

Confederate (kuhn-FED-ur-uht) a new part of the country formed when several states split from the Union

debt (DET) money or something else that someone owes

evacuated (i-VAK-yoo-a-ted) moved away from an area because of danger

infantry (IN-fuhn-tree) soldiers who fight on foot

militia (muh-LISH-uh) a group of people who are trained to fight but who aren't professional soldiers

probe (PROHB) to investigate or examine

reconciliation (reh-kun-sih-lee-AY-shuhn) a restoration of friendship and a settling of differences

siege (SEEJ) the surrounding of a place to cut off supplies

treason (TREE-zuhn) the crime of betraying one's country

trench warfare (TRENCH WAR-fare) fighting from long, narrow ditches that protect the soldiers

Union (YOON-yuhn) another name for the United States, or the name for the Northern states during the Civil War

Page numbers in *italics* indicate illustrations.

ABOUT THE AUTHOR

Peter Benoit is a graduate of Skidmore College in Saratoga Springs, New York. His degree is in mathematics. He has been a tutor and educator for many years. Peter has written more than two dozen books for Children's Press. He has written about ecosystems, disasters, and Native Americans, among other topics. He is also the author of more than 2,000 poems. He is fascinated by the Civil War.